A HEART SHAPED CANDY

and a Million Little Hands

MICHELLE GAUDET
ILLUSTRATED BY WENDY MORRISON

A HEART-SHAPED CANDY AND A MILLION LITTLE HANDS
Copyright © 2024 by Michelle Gaudet
Illustrated by Wendy Morrison

Scripture quotations marked (NLT) are taken from the Holy Bible, New Living Translation, copyright ©1996, 2004, 2015 by Tyndale House Foundation. Used by permission of Tyndale House Publishers, Carol Stream, Illinois 60188. All rights reserved. Scripture quotations marked (NIV) are taken from the Holy Bible, New International Version®, NIV®. Copyright © 1973, 1978, 1984, 2011 by Biblica, Inc.™ Used by permission of Zondervan. All rights reserved worldwide. www.zondervan. com The "NIV" and "New International Version" are trademarks registered in the United States Patent and Trademark Office by Biblica, Inc.™

ISBN: 978-1-4866-2583-3
eBook ISBN: 978-1-4866-2584-0

Word Alive Press
119 De Baets Street Winnipeg, MB R2J 3R9
www.wordalivepress.ca

WORD ALIVE
—PRESS—

Cataloguing in Publication information can be obtained from Library and Archives Canada.

"In reading Michelle's book, I felt as if I was there with her! I felt as if I was experiencing the very things that she was experiencing for the first time in a new land. She is gifted in expressing profound realities that we can all understand. Michelle's love for God and for others, through Jesus, is infectious. I highly recommend her book!"

—Ross Morrison
Pastor, Alberton Baptist Church

"*A Heart-Shaped Candy and a Million Little Hands* takes readers on a poignant journey across seven thousand miles, where amidst palm trees and hymns, amidst new faces and homemade toys, amidst shared smiles and sweet candies, Michelle discovers the profound blessings found in the simplicity and warmth of life's little moments, ultimately reaffirming her faith and igniting a soul-stirring transformation.

"What truly sets Michelle apart is her genuine desire to spread love wherever she goes by sharing her firsthand experiences in the Philippines. Her new book radiates warmth and compassion and leaves a lasting impression on everyone who reads it."

—Bernice Perry
Research Assistant, Saint Mary's University

"Michelle, I love your story. It's just beautiful. I can't seem to find the words, but it's like you've laid your heart open to give us a picture of your love for God and for His people, especially the little children! Thank you for sharing it with me early."

—Jeanne Clements
Vice President, Loving the Least of These Ministries International

"This heart-warming story was drawn from Michelle Gaudet's personal experiences as she served in the Philippines. She has beautifully captured the joy found in simple acts of giving and receiving. I am confident the readers will be enriched and inspired."

—Cindy Currin

And then he told them,

"Go into all the world and preach
the Good News to everyone."

(Mark 16:15, NLT)

For my friends in the Philippines
and my church family back home,
thank you for your love, prayer, and support.

For mission leader Anna
and the four youth who stole my heart,

Klient, Kycel, Vea, and Bles.

Seven thousand miles from home, surrounded by palm trees and bright, sunny weather, I step outside to be greeted by a woman in a long black dress. She speaks no words but wears a warm and sincere smile as she gently holds my hands.

Instantly I feel like I'm home.

As the sun rises, we gather around a fire, a tiny light shining in the early dawn. Waves crash along the beach as a guitar leads us through hymns and songs.

We sing in union, our hearts at peace. In awestruck wonder, we speak scriptures and tell stories, fellowshipping with one another as we share our hope with each other in faith, testifying to the love of our holy Father.

3

In the pew of a church, a pair of beautiful brown eyes glances back at me in curiosity. Another country, a different life. It is the sweetest smile, able to break through the language barrier.

That silent smile speaks more than a thousand words.

The service is starting! With eyes closed and hands outstretched to the sky, the little children pour out their hearts to God in song with beautiful voices. Oh how he loves when the little children sing! Music is the language of praise.

"I'm alive," we harmonize together. "I'm alive because he lives."

Though my ears can't understand at times, my heart bursts with joy as the pastor preaches the good news.

"He has risen!" he speaks in my language. "Jesus has risen from the grave!"

My soul soars from the manifested presence of the Lord that fills the church.

Listen! *Tip-tap, tip-tap...* the sounds of many little feet running my direction. The small children burst through the doors of the church, and to my surprise I am surrounded by many eager eyes staring up at me as I hold a big bag of heart-shaped candy.

There are no words to describe how I feel except these: a heart-shaped candy and a million little hands.

With grins on their faces, they share the sweet treats amongst themselves—for sharing is caring, and they do it quite well.

The children rush to the beach, jumping in the waves. They leap so high, tossing themselves into the ocean.

"This is the best day ever!" one boy shouts.

A good way to end the day.

11

Pausing in my tracks, I stop to watch the joy on a small boy's face. He skips and runs while pulling behind him a homemade toy car made of plastic and string. For children, luxury can be found in the simplest things.

The people around me extend greetings and welcomes, making new friends from many different walks of life. They reach out to shake hands, joy and warmth sowed upon their hearts.

Their lives are simple, uninterrupted by material distractions. Their young innocence is untainted by the world. The presence of God settles over them wherever they walk.

As the sun sets above the trees, I ponder my trip, remem-
bering the footsteps in the sand in a dream I once had.

I will follow.

So now you know: the greatest blessings are found in the
littlest things, the ones we sometimes pass by. Little things
become big things, just like the heart-shaped candy and
the million little hands.

I am the resurrection and the life.

The one who believes in me will live, even though they

die; and whoever lives by believing in me will never die.

Do you believe this?

(John 11:25–26, NIV)

Anna Gallant has dedicated herself to serving

God and her people of Palawan, Philippines.

She is a great mission trip leader in her church in Canada.

I, Michelle, am blessed to follow her guidance.

As always, she will say,

"All Glory To God".

www.ingramcontent.com/pod-product-compliance
Lightning Source LLC
Chambersburg PA
CBHW042109040426
42448CB00002B/198